STRATEGIC ROLE AND CHALLENGES OF DIPLOMATS IN FOREIGN POLICY MATTERS AND CONFLICT RESOLUTION: AMERICA'S HENRY KISSINGER IN PERSPECTIVE

ESTHER SAMSON

:

DEDICATION

To all diplomats who individually toil for their respective
nation's peace and progress, for world peace and security.
.

CONTENTS

ABSTRACT

Conflict is regarded as an inevitable aspect of human life. When allowed to become violent or war, it devastates lives, properties, and infrastructure; and diverts developmental resources to war fighting. Humanity in order to prevent war, or control it, if it inevitably breaks out, has established mechanisms such as Peace Support Operations. Peace Support Operations in themselves do not resolve conflicts. Rather, they provide the enabling atmosphere for negotiations to take place so that the root causes of the conflict can be removed and peace and social harmony restored. It is in these negotiations that diplomats are their best in their role, as well as in influencing and executing the foreign policy of their nations.

This modest piece examines the role of diplomats in foreign policy, and conflict prevention, management and resolution, highlighting the challenges that confront them, with particular reference to Henry Kissinger of the United States.

Key words: Strategic role, Challenges, diplomats, conflict resolution, Henry Kissinger, foreign policy.

PREAMBLE

Conflict is as old as human existence, and diplomacy, which has been a major strategic instrument of preventing, managing and resolving it has also been as old as man. The beginning of organized diplomacy, which is an instrument of foreign policy and conflict management in human history may be traced to ancient times, in the relations between the Greek City States such as Athens, Sparta, and other. As noted by Nicholson, by the fifth century, "special missions between the Greek City States had become so frequent that something approaching our own system of regular diplomatic intercourse had been achieved". There are also records by Thucydides about diplomatic procedures among Greeks, such as the Conference of Sparta in 432 BC during which Spartans and their allies strategised measures to be taken against Athens.

In the Eastern Roman Empire also, after Emperor Constantine moved his capital to Constantine, diplomatic techniques were deployed and employed with great impact. The Eastern Emperors for instance achieved great successes playing and paying off potential rivals against each other, putting into strategic use intelligence sent home by their Representatives in foreign courts. These Representatives were trained and skilled in accurate observation, and reporting in addition to their representative functions. Despite these, diplomacy, though had the content of representation, at the time was generally and more often seen as the study and preservation of achieves than the art of international negotiation. It was in the Papal and other chanceries that "the usage of diplomacy as a science based upon precedents and experience first came to be established" Thus, the Holy See and the Italian state evolved and developed systems of diplomacy at the early date and it is possible that the Holy See was the first to utilize the system of permanent representation which is a key feature of modern diplomacy. However, the first known permanent mission was that established by Francesco Sforza, the Duke of Milan in Genoa in 1455.

By the 17th century and more especially 18th century, diplomacy had become an established profession, with permanent missions, and a generally accepted mechanism of international intercourse, especially after the Peace of Westphalia of 1648 which crystallized and formalized the state system. Powerful rulers such as Peter the Great of Russia, and Frederick the Great of Prussia effectively used diplomacy backed up with military might when necessary to demand and achieve their goals. The Congress of Vienna 1815 that placed diplomacy on a more systematic and formal platform by laying down rules of procedure is still in use today.

Today, diplomacy enables the world to do its work, in interstate political and economic relations, providing the milieu for nations to carry on much of their formal business, policy, and international relations in peace and war. Through it, nations and governments seek to promote good relations among themselves, pursue their economic development, as well as export their culture and values.

The fundamental problem, however, is that the role of diplomats is not well known and adequately appreciated, especially in the present generation, and this ignorance has contributed to the challenges diplomats face in the pursuit of their noble and onerous duties. This ignorance and lack of adequate appreciation have also limited the number of people opting for a diplomatic career, thus making the field of diplomacy an all comers affair, rather than that of well trained, and skillful diplomats, especially in Africa.

The objectives of this paper are to examine the role of diplomats, and challenges confronting them with specific focus on Henry Kissinger. Several reasons justify this discourse at this point of Nigeria's national history. First,

STRATEGIC ROLE AND CHALLENGES OF DIPLOMATS IN FOREIGN POLICY MATTERS AND CONFLICT RESOLUTION:AMERICA'S HENRY KISSINGER INPERSPECTIVE

several of Nigeria's experts in our universities and research institutes are undervalued, and underutilized, unappreciated in the process of national development. So it is all over Africa. Many of them out of frustration have left for other nations where their values and expertise are appreciated and fully engaged. Henry Kissinger did not start contributing to US foreign policy and achievements when he became Secretary of State. His expertise was recognized, appreciated and put into the wheel of national service, progress and greatness while he was a lecturer in the University, and from there he blossomed to become an international star. The leaders of Nigeria and Africa should learn to identify and apply the great minds in our country and continent to great use.

Second, it is intended that this discourse will contribute to the preparatory knowledge of students and persons who wish to make a career in the field of diplomacy. Third, we believe that the role of diplomats in foreign policy shaping and implementation as well as conflict prevention, management, and resolution has not been given fair intellectual attention. Fourth, we believe that Nigerian, African, western world and other climes' serving and potential diplomats can see one or two things to learn from this modest paper focused on legendary Henry Kissinger his style, philosophy, patriotism, diligence, achievements, failures, and mistakes. Finally, this discourse is a humble tribute to all diplomats who individually toil for their respective nation's peace and progress, and for world peace and security

1
UNDERSTANDING CONCEPTS

It is deemed necessary here to define and discuss the concepts of conflict, conflict resolution, diplomacy, and diplomat to enhance the understating of this discourse.

Conflict

Conflict as a concept stems from the Latin word "conflictus" which stands for "clash". Thus, in its simple meaning, conflict is a clash of views, ideas, opinions, interests, personalities, groups, or nations. The Encyclopedia of the Social Sciences expresses conflict in its widest sense as a conscious competition in which the competitors become self-conscious rivals, opponents or enemies. For Abia, conflict means to come into collision or sharp disagreement with another party or parties over certain interests, ideas; or an altercation, the manifest clash between opposing forces, as well as to contend or do battle.

Louis Coser Conceptualizes conflict as:

"as struggle over and claims to scare resources in which the aims of opponents are to neutralize, injure or eliminate their rivals".

To some people, conflict has to be avoided, especially violent conflict because of its destructive and other negative potentials. However, to others, such as Burton, conflict is desirable as an essential creative element in human relationship. It is a means to change, and a means by which our social values of welfare, security, justice, and opportunities for personal development can be pursued and achieved. While we agree with the idea that conflict is destructive and have other negative consequences, we must also recognize its positive values as pointed out by Burton. The problem is that despots and other categories of bad leaders do not often effect reforms and changes seriously demanded by people and groups until violent conflict is applied. That is why colonialism and racism had to be challenged with violence in several nations before they were terminated, such as United States, Algeria, Angola, and South Africa. In the case of Nigeria today, if successive governments had done justice to the Niger Delta people, the issue of militancy, which has introduced kidnapping as a terror and money making technique into our national psyche would never have arisen.

Conflict Resolution

Conflict, especially violent conflict, can be monitored, and prevented from occurring. When it, however, occurs inevitably, it is managed and controlled to prevent it from escalating in intensity, and spreading in land area. This management and control may involve one or more **Peace Support Operations strategies such as observer mission, peacekeeping, peace enforcement, etc. While the management goes on, peace summits are organized by mediators, arbitrators, or reconciliators to enable the conflicting parties come together and identify and remove the causes of the conflict. This process involves negotiations which is the domain of seasoned diplomats, especially in international conflicts.** It is this removal of the real causes of conflict that is regarded as conflict resolution. Thus, when conflicts are terminated in the battlefield by one party triumphing over the other, or conflicts are frozen through the interposition of a mediating peace force, that is not conflict resolution.

Diplomacy

In its simple meaning, diplomacy is the use of wisdom, tact, and great skill in interacting with others. Sir Ernest Satow conceptualizes diplomacy as "the application of intelligence and tact to the conduct of official relations between the governments of independent states". This definition highlights the necessity of intelligence and tact in diplomatic functions, and underlines the fact that people to be appointed diplomats must be very intelligent and tactful persons. Henry Kissinger on his own asserts that diplomacy is:

The art by which peaceful intercourse between and among states is facilitated and conducted, and even when war breaks out, diplomacy is employed to facilitate the end of hostilities or to negotiate for a ceasefire or truce pending armistice and eventual peace protocol and signed peace.

A British diplomat once asserted that "foreign Policy is what you do, diplomacy is how you do it". One message here is that diplomacy is not just a purpose, or an end in itself, rather, it is a means or method. It uses reason, logic, mediation, conciliation, facilitation and exchange of interests, etc. to prevent serious conflicts from arising between sovereign nations. It seeks to achieve foreign policy goals through agreement instead of war.

In this direction, there are three key types of diplomacy:
Bilateral diplomacy, which focuses on relations between two nations or entities.
Multilateral diplomacy, which involves relations between

many nations, especially on the platform of an international organization such as the United Nations, African Union, ECOWAS, North Atlantic Treaty Organization, the European Union, etc.

Summitry diplomacy, which involves meetings and interactions of the occupants of the highest level of government, such as Presidents, Emperors, Queens, kings, and Prime Ministers. An example is the annual meeting of the G8 the leaders of the 8 wealthiest and most industrialized nations of the world which include USA, UK, Italy, Germany, France, Canada, and Japan.

Diplomat

Governments appoint their citizens to represent them in other countries, and carry out all diplomatic functions that concern their nations. These appointed representatives are regarded as diplomats, the chief of them is the Ambassador or High commissioner. Thus, a diplomat is essentially the man or woman appointed by his or her country to represent it and pursue its interests in another country. Before he takes off to the country of his appointment, he confers with his Head of State, Minister of Foreign Affairs, and other officials, and the diplomatic representatives in his country from the country of his assignment. He is also expected to study past relations between the two countries. While departing, he is issued with relevant papers, diplomatic passports for self and family, and letter of credence signed by his Head of State to be presented to the Head of State of his assignment on arrival, before his work begins as a diplomat.

THE ROLE, RIGHTS, PRIVILEGES, AND QUALITIES OF DIPLOMATS IN INTERSTATE RELATIONS

STRATEGIC ROLE AND CHALLENGES OF DIPLOMATS IN
FOREIGN POLICY MATTERS AND CONFLICT
RESOLUTION:AMERICA'S HENRY KISSINGER
INPERSPECTIVE

The Role of Diplomats

From the foregoing discourse, several roles of diplomats
have been implied. These general roles for emphasis
include Representation, Reporting, Negotiation, and
Protection of national interests. The specific roles of a
diplomat include:

Formal Representative of his country in a foreign state.

Normal agent of communication between his country and
his host nation.

Cultivating wide social contact with high ranking officials
in his host country, his own country and his fellow
diplomats, to facilitate his functions.

Effecting negotiations and bargaining when and where
necessary for achieving multilateral, bilateral or unilateral
treaties and agreements, including trade agreements, peace
agreements etc.

Serving as a key element in managing conflict and solving
problems that may arise between his country and host
country.

Pursuing economic diplomacy for his country externally.

Protecting his country's citizens, and business companies
and interests in his host country.

Effecting accurate observation over matters concerning his
country and reporting same home.

Serving as an agent of cross-cultural communication
between his government and country and his host
government and country.

Protecting, polishing, and promoting his government's and
country's external image.

Pursuing, protecting, and promoting the best interests of
his country in all spheres – political, economic, social,
technological, environmental, spiritual, cultural, etc. This
role is seen as the bedrock of diplomacy. In this, he assists
and protects businessmen, seamen, students, sports and
games teams, and cultural troupes from his country. He

prevents or corrects practices in host country that seem to discriminate against his own country's citizens.

Promotion of peaceful and cordial relations between his country and host country.

Rights And Privileges of Diplomats In Host Nations

To be able to play their role effectively in their host nations, it is general practice to accord diplomats, certain rights and privileges in their host nations. These include:

Enjoyment of Immunity not granted to private citizens, as diplomats are representatives of nations.

Freedom from restrictions imposed by local laws of the host nation.

Exemption from direct taxes.

Exemption from customs duties.

Exemption from civil and criminal prosecution.

Exemption from most of the laws of the host nation generally.

Inviolability of their persons, families, staff, and premises.

Qualities of A Diplomat

For a diplomat to be effective and successful, he needs to possess qualities that include:

Excellent knowledge of human nature, and host nation.

Power of oratory, and shrewdness.

Quick reasoning, logical thinking, and quick intelligence.

Power of hard bargaining negotiation skills.

Possession of excellent moral character and ability to comport oneself with decorum, because his country will be assessed and judged according to the personal impression he makes in his host nation.

Being highly sociable.

Capable of long and tedious sitting.

Ability to represent the best of his nation's character and culture.

Possession of excellent knowledge of his country, people

and their culture.

Being courageous and capable of giving leadership, and good advice.

Being security conscious at all times and places.

Possessing the ability to perform the tasks of a seasoned diplomat,

Good dressing.

Astute peacemaker, mediator, arbitrator, conciliator, and communicator,

Capable of commanding respect.

.

2
HENRY KISSINGER: LIFE, ROLE IN FOREIGM POLICY AND CONFLICT RESOLUTION

Overview of Henry Kissinger's Life

Henry Kissinger was born in 1923 to Jewish parents, Louis and Paula Kissinger, in Furth, Germany, and named Heinz Alfred Kissinger. The Surname was taken by his great grandfather Meyer Lob in 1817 from the city of Bad Kissingen 11. His name was changed to Henry in 1938 in New York when his parents flee from Nazi persecution as Heinz was too German. He nationalized as a United States citizen in 1943, while in the military training camp in South Carolina.

His high school years were spent in the Washington Heights' section of Upper Manhattan.12 He also attended George Washington High School at night, and worked in a shaving brush factory in the day. While in City College of New York, he was drafted into the U.S. Army in 1943, trained at Clemson College in South Carolina, and became a German interpreter for the 970th Counter Intelligence

Corps, rising there to the rank of Sergeant.

Kissinger received his First degree at Harvard College in 1950, his Masters and Doctorate degree at Harvard University in 1952 and 1954 respectively13. In 1952, he served as a Consultant to the Director of the Psychological Strategy Board. He remained at Harvard after his Ph.D. in the Department of Government, and at the Centre of International Affairs. In 1955, he became Consultant to National Security Council's Operating Co-ordinating Board.14 From 1955 to 1956, he served as Study Director in Nuclear Weapons and Foreign Policy at the Council of Foreign Relations. Between 1958 and 1971, he worked for the Rockefeller Brother's Fund as Director of Special Duties Program.

He was a Consultant to several government agencies such as **Operations-Research** Office, and Arms Control and Disarmament Agency. He was adviser to Nelson Rockefeller, Governor of New York, who sought for the Republican Party's Presidential ticket thrice between 1960 and 1968.

Kissinger's major breakthrough came when Richard Nixon won the Presidency in 1968, and appointed him National Security Adviser. Since this appointment, he had several others in the US government, all of which enabled him to bestride governments and exert great influence on public policies especially US Foreign policies over several years like a Colossus.

Kissinger married his first wife Ann, with whom he had two children, Elizabeth and David, but they divorced in 1964, paving way for his second marriage to Nancy in 1973.

Ill-health came in 1982, leading to his having triple coronary bypass heart surgery in May._Kissinger is a soccer fan, and is a supporter and honorary member of the German soccer club Spielvereiniung Greuther Furth of his home town, and to which he belonged in his youth.

Kissinger is widely traveled. He is one of the most loved, and most hated American Secretaries Ministers depending on one's bearing, based on his foreign police roles, advice and influence; especially over the Middle East crisis, the Vietnam war, Cuban crisis, US – Africa relations, US – China relations, US-Soviet Union relations, the role of America in Chile especially as it concerns the overthrow of President Allende Gossins by the military junta led by General Pinochet, and others. Over the Chilean problem, and some others there have been attempts to sue and prosecute Kissinger.

In 1973, Kissinger was awarded the Nobel Peace Prize along with North Vietnamese Le Duc Tho especially for their role in negotiating the ceasefire that led to the Paris Peace Accord which laid foundation for the end of the Vietnam War. He became an honorary citizen of Furth, Germany, where he was born in 1998. In 2006, he received the prestigious Woodrow Wilson award for Public Service. In 2007, he received the Hophins Nanjing Award for his role in re-establishing Sino-American relations

Shortly after leaving office in 1976, Kissinger was offered an endowed Chair at Columbia University in 1977. But some students petitioned against his appointment charging him of illegal actions in Vietnam, Cambodia, and Chile among others. He was hounded and humiliated by his students who dogged his initial classes and meetings. The appointment was dropped, and Kissinger went to Georgetown University, where the students were less antagonistic. In 2001, Nichens wrote his damning book: The Trial of Henry Kissinger, criticizing his policy towards Vietnam, Cyprus, Cambodia, Chile, and East Pakistan, and Kissinger became a focal point of criticisms from NGOs, and Human Rights Groups.

He is today head of Kissinger Associates, a consulting firm, through which he has remained relevant in the

private and public life in the United States. Before
President Barak Obama assumed office after his election,
he sent Kissinger to Moscow to discuss nuclear stockpile
reduction with the Russian President.   He is also a
Television Commentator, and a Lecturer.

Henry Kissinger's Foreign Policy And Conflict Resolution Roles: Selected Cases

The Vietnam War:

Henry Kissinger's role in U.S. Foreign Policy and Conflict
resolution began even before his appointment as National
Security Adviser by President Nixon in 1966. While at
Harvard University, he served as a consultant on foreign
policy in the White House and State Department. For
example, he was empowered by his old friend who was an
Ambassador in Saigon to tour Vietnam in 1965 and 1966,
which visit made him see the futility of United States'
military victories, and necessity for ultimate withdrawal.
Kissinger thus played deep role in the withdrawal of
American forces from Vietnam, and the end of the
Vietnam war. In 1967, he went on a peace initiative,
mediating between Washington and Hanoi. President
Nixon was elected in 1968 on the promise of achieving
"Peace with honour", and ending the Vietnam war.
Kissinger assisted the President in achieving this goal.

US-Soviet Detent

Kissinger, who is a proponent of realpolitik, played a
dominant role in US foreign policy especially between
1968 and 1977. One of his key areas of focus was US-
Soviet relations. In this period, he expounded the policy of
detent, which led to a significant relaxation in US-Soviet
tensions. Within this framework of détente, he negotiated
the strategic Arms Limitations Treaty, SALT, and the Anti-
Ballistic Missile Treaty with Soviet authorities.

US-China Relations

The expertise and efforts of Kissinger led in 1971 to closer ties between the US and China. The policy of detent enabled talks between US and Chinese leaders. These talks led to a rapprochement between the US and People's Republic of China; and to the formulation of a new strategy of anti-Soviet Sino-American alliance. This paved the way for the ground breaking 1972 Summit between President Nixon of US, and Premier Zhou and Chairman Moa Zedong both of China. This Summit led to the formalization of relations between the US and China, ending 23 years of diplomatic isolation, and mutual hostility. Liaison offices were established in the capitals of both countries, and economic and cultural exchanges were stimulated. Full normalization of relations, however, occurred in 1979, opening up China to the West. This opening up of China is one of Kissinger's greatest achievements.

Indo-Pakistan War

Under Henry Kissinger's guidance, the United States government supported Pakistan in the Indo-Pakistan war of 1971. Kissinger was particularly concerned with the threat of Soviet expansionism in South Asia as a result of the treat of friendship signed at the period by India and the Soviet Union. Kissinger and the US government wanted to demonstrate to China, - ally of Pakistan, and enemy of India and USSR the relevance of alliance with the USA.16 In those hey days of East-West cold war, US support for Pakistan, and hot US-India altercations, Kissinger described the Prime Minister of India, Mrs. Indira Gandhi as a bitch17, a comment he later expressed regrets over.18 The US has remained a strong ally of Pakistan till date, not minding whether the country is under military dictatorship or not.

Middle-East: 1973 Yom Kippur War

The Middle-East crises began with the creation of the state of Israel in 1948; and has given rise to several wars between Israel and her Arab neighbours especially Egypt, Syria, Jordan, and Lebanon since then. In 1973, Israel was invaded again by some of her neighbours mainly Egypt and Syria, in what came to be called the Yom Kippur War, during which Israel lost grounds within a few days of the attack. The United States to avoid the humiliation and overrunning of Israel, conducted the largest military airlift in history within a few days. The huge logistics support for Israel enabled her to regain the territory lost in the early fighting, and also go on the offensive to sack the invading enemy forces and capture new territories in Syria and Egypt.

Henry Kissinger played key role in ensuring quick US support, and in negotiating an end to the Yom Kippur war. He also was deeply influential to the decision of Israel handing some of the captured Egyptian land back to Egypt which laid foundation for the latter closer US-Egypt relations, and Israeli-Egyptian non-aggression peace pact. The peace pact was finalized in 1978 when President Jimmy Carter mediated the Camp David Accords through which Israel returned the Sinai Peninsular to Egypt in exchange for Egypt's recognition of the state of Israel.

US-Cuba Relations

United States relations with Cuba were broken in 1961 with the emergence of socialist government of Fidel Castro which leaned towards the Communist Soviet Union. The 1962 Curban Missile Crisis worsened matters as all US-Cuba trade was blocked. Out of US pressure, Cuba was expelled from the Orgnistion of American States

OAS.
Henry Kissinger was initially supportive of the idea of normalizing US-Cuba relations, but seeing the way the US-thought pendulum was swinging, he abandoned the idea.

CIA-Backed Military Coup In Chile

Salvador Allende Gossin in 1970 became the first socialist President to be popularly elected in United States backyard. This development caused serious political and ideological concern in the USA. This was more so because President Gossin manifested strong pro-Castro tendencies. Probably fearing further multiplication of socialist governments among OAS members, the Nixon government authorized the Central Intelligence Agency CIA to engineer a military coup to prevent Gossin's inauguration, but the plan failed.19
Kissinger's involvement in these plans remains a subject of controversy, but it is clear that he was alleged to be involved in the plans that culminated in the murder of General Rene Schneider of Chile who was vehemently opposed to a military coup against Gossin's government. The CIA under the influence of Kissinger provided information and education for the Chilean military officers who were directly involved in the coup against Allende Gossin,20 provided funds for the stage-managed anti-government strikes in 1972 and 1973 building up to Allende's overthrow and death. During the period, Kissinger made several controversial statements against Gossin's government even to the point of openly canvassing US intervention, and judging the Chilean people irresponsible and incapable of managing their affairs. In his words:
the issues are much too important for the Chilean voters to be left to decide for themselves and I don't see why we

need to stand by and watch a country go communist due
to the irresponsibility of its people.21

These remarks sparked outrage among many
commentators who considered them too patronizing and
disparaging of Chile's democracy, and sovereignty. In his
anger against Communism, he crucified the right of the
Chilean people to self-determination, and made U.S.A. the
sole determinant of their fate. These statements hunt him
along others to-date.

US And The Angolan Civil War

Kissinger carried the same attitude he displayed over Chile
to Angola. In 1974, a leftist military coup overthrew the
government of Caetano in Portugal, and granted
independence to Portugal's colonies. This was a boost to
the aim of the then Organization of African Unity OAU of
ridding Africa of colonialism, racism, and racist minority
regimes. But it now pitched the OAU and Cuban-backed
Left-wing Popular Movement for the Liberation of Angola
MPLA led by Augustino Neto in ferocious war against the
US and South African backed UNITA and FNLA rebels in
an ensuing war 1975-2002. Kissinger ignored Africa's
position, and the support of most Angolans for the
MPLA, and moved the US and its allies to support FNLA
led by Holden Roberto, and UNITA led by Jonas
Savombi. Kissinger was however among the forces that
pressurized the Rhodesian Prime Minister, Ian Smith to
quicken the transition of power to black majority rule.

Achievements, Failures and Challenges

Henry Kissinger like any other astute diplomat made
remarkable achievements. He also had his failures,
mistakes, and challenges. Among his outstanding

achievements are his rise to the post of Secretary of State; and the opening up of China to Western ideas and influence. He laid the foundation for the reception and presence of Western businesses and cultures in China today. He also pioneered and midwifed the US-USSR detent policy as National Security Adviser to Nixon, and successfully negotiated the SALT I.

He served as occasional foreign policy adviser to several US Presidents like Dwight Eisenhower, John Kennedy, and Lyndon Johnson. Kissinger also effected strategic and foreign policy studies for several US governments. He was and remains very influential in the formulation and implementation of US foreign policy. He accompanied President Nixon to China and USSR in 1972, and represented US in negotiations towards the settlement of the Indochina war in 1971.

The agreement that led to the establishment of ceasefire in the Vietnam war in 1973 was essentially out of his efforts, and for this he shared the 1973 Nobel Peace Prize with the North Vietnamese diplomat, Le Duc Tho.

Kissinger is the first foreign born US citizen to be appointed Secretary of State in the United States. After serving in that capacity under President Nixon, he was retained by President Ford, an act that showed the recognition and appreciation of his professional expertise. He negotiated a disengagement agreement between Israel and Egypt in 1975, using a method of diplomacy expressed as "shuttle diplomacy".22 His effort led to the Geneva Peace Process in 1977.

He contributed immensely in the designing of the Nixon Doctrine which aimed to soften the hard edges of the US containment strategy. He had successful disengagement diplomacy in the 1973 Middle East war by Separating Egyptian, Israeli and Syrian forces.

Kissinger was awarded the United States Presidential Medal for freedom in 1977, and the United States Medal of Liberty in 1986. He has several books, journal articles, speeches, address, and policy papers to his credit from the platforms he occupied as a University lecturer, foreign policy and strategic studies consultant, President's National Secretary Adviser, and Secretary of State Minister.

Henry Kissinger experienced a number of failures as a Diplomat. For example, he laboured without success to arrange a racial settlement in Southern Africa, especially in Rhodesia now Zimbabwe. He could not also translate into reality and effective action his initial preference and support for the normalization of US-Cuba relations broken in 1961.

He stuck to the philosophy of realpolitik, and could not see the moral wrongs and injustices brought about by US foreign policies in different parts of the world especially in Latin America Chile, Middle-East and Africa Angola, South Africa etc.

The mistakes of Henry Kissinger as a diplomat include: His inability to see merit in Africa's positions on various continental issues due to his perception of such issues from communist prism and US interests. In this direction, he sacrificed Africa's interests and is today not in the good books of most Africans: His support for right wing coupists who unpatriotically sacrificed their people's interests in promotion of US interests e.g. General Pinochet in Chile. His support for despots and right wing rulers and organizations that violated human rights and murdered several citizens, as long as they were useful in oiling US interests and anti-Soviet Cold War machine e.g. apartheid governments in South Africa, UNITA and FNLA in Angola, and CIA supported invasion of Angola by apartheid South African Forces. He has been linked to some assassinations, murder, disappearances, and conspiracy in Chile, Bangladesh, East Timor, Cyprus, Greece, Indonesia, and other countries. This has made some people to call for his arrest and trial for war crimes.23 On memorial Day in 2001, Henry Kissinger was served a warrant by the Police in Ritz Hotel, in Paris, issued by Judge Roger Leloire seeking his testimony over the disappearance of Certain French citizens in Chile under General Augusto Pinochet planted in office by CIA with Kissinger's influence. Henry Kissinger rather than respecting the Court in Paris, decided to leave town. **His strong protection** of General Augusto Pinochet from prosecution for murder, assassination, and human rights abuses, when Jews till date are still haunting down nazists that killed their people during World War II. **His support for illegal** financial and military aid for the invasion of nations like Cyprus; execution of coups that overthrew popularly elected governments like Allende Gossin's government in Chile, and dirty wars in Argentina in the 1970 which led to over 30, 000 deaths.24 **He also insulted and embarrassed leaders** of sovereign nations, such as his referring to the Prime Minister of India, Mrs. Indira Gandhi as a bitch.

Henry Kissinger faced a lot of challenges some of which contributed to his failures and mistakes. For example, as a government man and patriotic American citizen, he had to pursue official policies and national interests even where they were against his personal belief and conscience. Again, often, he came face to face with world public opinion and conscience that challenged his actions and the policies of the government he served.

There were also several moments of risk, threats and danger to his life. For example, while on one of the many flights he took in search of peace in the Middle East, five terrorists in Beirut were detailed by an Arab Leader to shoot down the plane carrying Kissinger for the peace conference. On many instances too, government preferred to use force instead of waiting for the slow moving diplomatic process.

3
RECENT CONFLICTS AND HOW KISSINGER'S DIPLOMATIC METHODS WOULD HAVE MADE AN IMPACT

THE IRAQ WAR

The Iraq was called Second Persian Gulf War. Iraq's invasion of Kuwait in 1990 ended in Iraq's defeat by the U.S led coalition in the Persian Gulf War.

However, the Iraqi branch of the Ba'th Party, headed by Saddam Hussein, managed to retain power by harshly suppressing uprisings of the country's minority Kurds and majority Shiite Arabs.

Moreover, to retain future Iraqi aggression, the United Nations implemented economic sanctions against Iraq in order to, among other things hinder the progress of its most lethal arms programs, including those for the development of nuclear, biological and chemical weapons.

UN inspections during the mid-1990s uncovered a variety of weapons of mass destruction and prohibited technology throughout Iraq. They received many UN weapons ban and its continuous interference with the inspections frustrated the international community and led U.S then president Bill Clinton in 1998 to order the bombing of several Iraqi military installations **CODE-NAMED OPERATION DESERT FOX**. After the bombing Iraq refused to allow inspectors to reenter the country and during the next several years the economic sanctions slowly began to erode as neighbouring countries sought to trade with Iraq.

In 2002 when the new U.S president George W. Bush argued that the Iraqi government under the rule of Saddam Hussein support al-Qaeda who were the perpetrators of the September 11 attacks and were in continued possession and manufacture of weapons of mass destruction made disarming Iraq a renewed priority.

UN Security Council Resolution 1441, passed on November 8, 2002 demanded that Iraq allow inspectors and that it comply with all previous resolutions.

Iraq appeared to comply with all previous resolutions, but in early 2003 President Bush and British Prime Minister Tony Blair declared that Iraq was actually continuing to hinder UN inspectors and that it still retained its weapons of mass destruction. Other world leaders such as the former French President Jacques Chirac, German Chancellor Gerhard Schröder saw the cooperation from the Iraqi government and sought to extend inspections and give Iraq more time to comply with them.

However, on March 17 2003 seeking no further UN resolutions and deeming further diplomatic efforts by the Security Council was not making any progress, Bush declared an end to diplomacy and issued an ultimatum to Saddam, giving the Iraqi president 48 hours to leave Iraq. The leaders of France, Germany, Russia, and other countries objected to the war, but President Bush still went ahead with his decision to use military intervention.

When Saddam Hussein refused to leave Iraq, U.S and allied forces launched an attack and dropped several bombs and a series of air strikes directed against the

government and military installations and within days U.S,
forces had invaded Iraq.

In 2003 after so much resistance, Saddam Hussein was
captured on December 13, 2003 and was turned over to
the Iraqi authorities in June 2004 to stand trial for various
crimes against humanities.

The so-called dictator was overthrown through military
intervention and it is obvious that this method did not
solve the problem in Iraq, nor ensure peace in the country,
instead it led to an outbreak of violence, which escalated
into a civil war between the Shiite-Sunni tribe.

The Shiite feel marginalized and the Iraqi's Kurdish
minority on the other hand, enjoys strong autonomy in the
north of the country, with its own government and
security forces.

Despite the transfer of power and evacuation of the
American troops in December 2011.

A once beautiful, peaceful and prosperous country is today
in a devastating state of instability. There is a high rate of
unemployment, extremist's groups like the ISIS has seized
much of the northwestern Iraq and adjacent parts of Syria
and to top it all there is a growing refugee crisis.

I believe that if the world leaders and former leaders of the
United States had applied some of Henry Kissinger's
diplomatic policies of "Detent and Shuttle Diplomacy"
maybe this war would have been averted. This would have
enabled strong negotiations with neighbouring Arab
leaders, allowing them to come together to formulate some
strategies, which would help remove Saddam Hussein and
replace him with a more suitable leader instead of relying
on military intervention, which has also led to the death of
many civilians and American soldiers.

Iraq is a sovereign country and should be free from any
kind of intervention. Therefore, declaring an end to
diplomacy and not extending the inspections or giving the

Iraqi government more time to comply would have saved Iraq from chaos, America a lot of revenue, criticism and casualties.

THE UKRAINE WAR

The war in Ukraine is an armed conflict in the Donbass region of Ukraine. From the beginning of March 2014, demonstrations by the pro-Russian and anti-government groups took place in the Donetsk and Luhansk oblasts of Ukraine, together commonly called the "Donbass", in the aftermath of the 2014 Ukrainian revolution and the Euromaidan movement. These demonstrations, which followed the annexation of Crimea by the Russian Federation, and which were part of a wider group of concurrent pro-Russian protests across southern and eastern Ukraine, escalated into an armed conflict between the separatist forces of the self-declared Donetsk and Luhansk people's Republics DPR and LPR.

In August, Russian artillery, personnel, and what Russia called a "humanitarian convoy" were reported to have crossed the border into Ukrainian territory without the permission of the Ukrainian government. Crossings were reported to have occurred both in areas under the control of pro-Russian forces and areas that were not under their control, such as the southeastern part of Donetsk Oblast, near Novoazovsk. This resulted in the invasion of Ukraine by Russia.

The DPR and LPR insurgents regained much of the territory they had lost during the preceding government military offensive. A deal to establish a ceasefire, called the Minsk Protocol, was signed on 5 September 2014. Violations of the ceasefire on both sides were common, and this led to renewed fighting across the conflict zone, including at Donetsk International Airport and Debaltseve and forced Ukrainian forces to withdraw from it.

During the crisis, we saw how it affected the import and export of goods, business investments between the European countries as well as Ukraine and Russia.

It led to a spike in inflation and the death of many like the crash of the Malaysian Airline, which flew across the Ukrainian Airspace.

The European Union strongly condemned the illegal annexation of Crimea by Russia, and carried out certain diplomatic measures like placing an embargo on import and export of arms and freezing assets of individuals from Russia abroad, not allowing European cruise ships to dock in the Crimean Peninsula, stopping any further bilateral talks between Russia and the European Union.

However, it is very clear that Russia broke international law and violated Ukrainian sovereignty by involving itself in the war. Its military intervention and continuous support of foreign fighters with weapons and ammunition worsen the situation.

The supply of weapons to the Kiev government by the American government also added more fuel to the issue. Instead, they would have encouraged continuous dialogue between both countries just like Kissinger did to end the Yom Kippur war of 1976. This would have helped to resolve the matter quickly.

THE BOKO HARAM INSURGENCY

Before the colonization and annexation into the British Empire in 1900 as colonial Nigeria, the Bornu Empire ruled the territory where Boko Haram is presently active. The Kanuri Muslim dominated this region. In 1903, both the Borno Emirate and Sokoto Caliphate came under the control of the British. Christian missionaries spread their message in the region and had many converts. After the Nigerian independence in 1960, there were Ethnic militancy called the Yan Tatsine group, who started riots that resulted in the death of more than 4,000 people at that time.

Maitatsine was killed, but his radical doctrine was preserved by many in the northern area especially in Kano State.

The term "Boko Haram" means Western is forbidden. It opposes the Western education, culture. The group was founded in 2002 in Maiduguri by Mohammed Yusuf, who was influenced by the Wahhabi theology, which is described as pure and hopes of change to the Caliphate Islamic religion. It is a movement of revolutionary Jihad. Mohammed Yusuf established a religious complex and school that attracted poor Muslim people from across Nigeria and other States. His aim was to create an Islamic state, and become a recruiting ground for the Jihadis. He started the Izala society, which was accepted by the government and started its activities peacefully for seven years before it became violent.

In 2004 it moved to Kanamma, Yobe State, where it set up a base called "Afghanistan", used to attack nearby police outposts, killing police officers.

After the death of Mohammed Yusuf, Abubakar Shekau a man described as a criminal, fearless psychopath became the leader of Boko Haram and is more radical. He speaks Arabic, Kanuri, Hausa and as a result, it is easy for him to communicate with the other extremist groups abroad.

Boko Haram gets funds from bank robberies and ransoms from kidnapping.

For example, in 2013, some Boko Haram militants kidnapped a family of seven French tourists and 16 others on vacation in Cameroon. They had to pay $3.15 million before they were released. They also receive donations from wealthy Nigerian citizens who believe in their ideologies.

Boko Haram has attacked churches, military camps, mosques, UN headquarters in Abuja.

They have their base in the Sambisa forest and the

Mandara mountains, close to the border with Cameroon.

They have launched attacks on nearby villages, killing many children and women.

The worst was when they abducted 200 Christian school girls from Chibok town in Borno State to sell them as slaves. The group also pledges allegiance to the militant group Islamic State and have killed more than 10,000 people.

The present Nigerian president Mohammed Buhari had a dialogue with the Cameroonian president Paul Biya and other countries like, Chad, Niger, Benin to form a joint Task force of about 8,700 troops and as a result many militants have been killed and villages recovered.

I am very happy with the steps that the present Nigerian government has taken to stop Terrorism in Nigeria but we should ask ourselves this question "will only military intervention be effective for a long time"?

I think the government should hold talks to tackle this problem from its root, which would ensure a lasting and peaceful country. For example, there are intelligent diplomats like Professor Osisioma B.C. Nwolise, Emeka Ezegou and so many others, whose diplomatic theories might also help to solve this problem. I was born in Kano state, where most of these riots first started. These religious fundamentalists pick up young Hausa street kids called **"DANDOKO"**, manipulate them and end up sending them to the streets to do their dirty work.

Therefore, the Nigerian government need to invest more in education, creating jobs and building hostels for these kids in the north because most of them come from very poor background and are homeless, that is why they fall victim to groups like the Boko Haram. For example, there is plenty of farm land in these areas and these children could be taught how to farm or weave baskets, make groundnut oil, learn how to create craft or wooden works

which they can sell at the market to generate less income.
I watched a video of the Boko Haram and saw that they are well equipped with sophisticated weapons, armored cars.
We should then ask ourselves "How do they smuggle these weapons into the country?" More investments need to be made in our local intelligence agency to intercept any source of foreign support they might be receiving from other terrorist groups abroad and private individuals.

THE SECOND LIBYAN CIVIL WAR

The second Libyan civilian war is an ongoing conflict between four rival organizations seeking to control Libya: The internationally recognized government of the Council of Deputies that was elected democratically in 2014, also known as the "Tobruk government" and internationally known formally as the "Libyan Army under the command of General officer Khalifa Haftar and has been supported by airstrikes by Egypt and the UAE: the rival Islamist government of the General National Congress based in the capital Tripoli, led by the Muslim Brotherhood, backed by the wider Islamist coalition known as "Libya Dawn" and aided by Qatar, Sudan and Turkey: the Islamist Shura Council of Benghazi Revolutionaries, led by Ansar al-Sharia in Libya, which has had the support of the General National Congress and the unrecognized government in Tripoli led by former Prime Minister Omar Al-Hassi, stating that Ansar al-Sharia are simple, beautiful and amicable as well as being engaged in missionary work.
There are also two smaller organizations seeking to control small parts of Libya: The Tuareg militants of Ghat, controlling desert areas in the southwest; and the local forces in Mistrata district, controlling the towns of Bani Walid and Tawergha.
At the beginning of 2014, Libya was governed by the

General National Congress GNC after the election of
2012. Since then, Islamist parties had controlled the
assembly, taking over the majority centrists and liberals,
and electing Nouri Abusahmain as president of the GNC
in June 2013.

Many have said that Nouri abused his power to suppress
debates and inquiries.

In December 2013, the GNC voted to enforce a variant of
sharia law and decided to extend its 18-month mandate for
a year until the end of 2014, in a coup attempt, General
Khalifa Hafar, served under the former regime of
Muammar Gaddafi, called on the GNC to dissolve and for
the formation of a caretaker government committee to
oversee new elections. In May 2014, forces loyal to
General Haftar launched a large scale air and ground
attacks codenamed "**OPERATION DIGNITY**" against
Islamist armed groups in Benghazi and against the GNC in
Tripoli. In June, the GNC called for new elections to a
Council of Deputies: Islamists were defeated, but rejected
the results of the election, which saw only an 18% turnout.

The conflict escalated on 13 July 2014, when Tripoli's
Islamists and Mistratan militans launched Operation Libya
Dawn to seize Tripoli International Airport, capturing it
from the Zintan militia on 23 August. Later, members of
the General National Congress, whom had rejected the
June election came together and voted themselves as
replacement of the newly elected Council of Deputies,
with Tripoli as their political capital, Nouri Abusahmain as
president and Omar al-Hasi as prime minister.

The majority of the Council of Deputies was forced to
relocate to Tobruk, aligning itself with Haftar's forces and
eventually nominating him army chief.

On 6 November, the supreme court in Tripoli dominated
by the new GNC, declared the Council of Deputies
dissolved.

On 16 January 2015, Operation Dignity and Libya Dawn factions agreed on a ceasefire. The country is now led by two separate governments, with Tripoli and Misrata controlled by forces loyal to Libya Dawn and the new GNC in Tripoli. The international community recognizes Abdullah al-Than's government and its parliament in Tobruk. Benghazi remains a contest between pro Haftar forces and radical Islamists.

THE SYRIAN WAR

Syria became an independent republic in 1946 and there has been two more military coups that same year. The Ba'ath Syrian Regional Branch government came to power through a successful coup d'état in 1963. Another coup in 1966 overthrew Michel Aflaq and Salah al-Din AL Bitar:

General Hafez al-Assad, the Minister of Defense, came into power in November 1970, becoming Prime Minister. In March 1971, Hafez Assad, an Alawite, declared himself President, a position that he held until his death in 2000.

Since 1970, the secular Syrian Regional Branch has remained the dominant political authority in what had been a one-party state until the first multi-party election to the people's Council of Syria was held in 2012. The regime survived many revolts by Sunni Islamists until 1982.

In 2000, Bashar al-Assad took over as president of Syria upon Hafez al-Assad's death. He and his wife Asma al-Assad, a Sunni Muslim born and educated in Britain, initially inspired hopes for democratic reforms. Bashar Assad had failed to deliver on promised reforms. The country banning public gathering of more than five people, and effectively granting security forces sweeping powers of arrest and detention. Rights of free expression, association, and assembly were strictly controlled in Syria. The authorities harass and imprison human rights activities and other critics of the government, who are often indefinitely detained and tortured in poor prison conditions. Women and ethnic minorities have faced discrimination in the public sector. Thousands of Syrian Kurds were denied citizenship in 1962 and their descendants continued to be labeled as foreigners. Pro-democracy protests erupted in March 2011 in the southern city of Deraa after the arrest and torture of some teenagers who painted revolutionary slogans on a school wall.

After security forces opened fire on demonstrators, killing several more took to the street. The unrest triggered nationwide protests demanding president Assad's resignation.

The government's use of force to crush the protesters merely hardened the protesters. By July 2011, hundreds of thousands were taking to the street across the country.

Opposition supporters eventually began to take up arms, first to defend themselves and later to expel security forces from their local areas. The Assad government opposed the US invasion of Iraq in 2003 and the Bush administration undertook to destabilize the regime by increasing sectarian tensions, showcasing and publicizing Syrian repression of radical Kurdish and Sunni groups and financing political dissidents. In addition, Assad opposed the Qatar- Turkey pipeline in 2009. Violence escalated and the country descended into civil war as rebel's brigades were formed to battle government forces for central of cities, towns and the countryside.

Fighting reached the capital Damascus and second city Aleppo in 2012

A classified 2013 report by a joint U.S army intelligence group concluded to bring down Assad would have drastic consequences, since the opposition supported by the Obama administration was dominated by Jihadist.

More than 250,000 Syrians have lost their lives in four and half years of armed conflict, which began with anti-government protests before escalating into a full scale civil war. More than 11 million others have been forced from their home as forces loyal to president Bashar al-Assad and those opposed to his rule battle with each other- as well as Jihadist militants from the Islamic State.

The Syrian war has negative effects, which has affected both its citizens, neighbouring countries and the world at large especially Europe.

There has been a high death rate of children, men and women.

Many families have been displaced causing sorrow, strive and hunger.

There has been an increase in crime. For example, smugglers are using this medium to exploit these refugees financially. Many of them end up being sold into slavery, or to organ traffickers.

It has also affected trade between neighbouring countries like Lebanon. The war has reduced demand for goods and services, including impact on exporters of manufactured goods from minerals and fuels.

RUSSIAN TIES WITH SYRIA AND IT'S FIGHT AGAINST ISIS

Syria was an ally to the Soviet Union during the cold war and this resulted in a strong political bond. Between 1955 and 1958, Syria received about $ 294 million from the Soviet Union for military and economic assistance. The Suez War in 1956 increased a multiplication of relationship between Syria and the Soviet Union, and as a result increase the influence of the Syrian Ba'ath Party.

The Syrian Revolution of February 1966 gave the Soviet Union the opportunity to further support Syria. In 1971, under an agreement with the Syrian Ba'athist government's president Hafez al-Assad, the Soviet Union was allowed to open its naval military base in Tartus, giving the Soviet Union a stable presence in the Middle East.

Due to this strong relationship, Russia started series of air strikes on 30 September 2015 in places around the cities of Homs and Hama, targeting Syria's main opposition. Russian warplanes attacked rebel positions in al-Rastan,

Talbiseh and Zafaraniya in Homs province, Aydoun, a
village on the outskirts of the town of Slamiya: Deer Foul,
between Hama and oms and the outskirts of Salmiya.

Most of the initial airstrikes targeted positions of Chechen
fighters, Islamic Front's Jaysh al-Islam and the Free Syrian
Army.

During a Russian Airstrike in October 2015, an ISIS
command and control center was destroyed in a single
attack in Al-Qaryatayn, while an ISIS convoy on their way
to the Teefor-Palmyra highway was also attacked.
Following the airstrikes, the Syrian Army and National
Defence Forces pushed ISIS out of the town of Mheen
towards Al-Qaryatayn after a two-hour fight that killed 18
militants and destroyed two technical mounted with deadly
weapons. Syrian forces then started a counter south-west
of Al-Qaryatayn ro recover the main road.

On the same day, the Russian Air Force began bombing
Al-Nusra Front positions in al-Rastan and Talbiseh in the
Homs province. Later they bombed Al-Nustra in Kafr
Zita, Al-Ghaab plains, Kafr Nabl, Kafr Sijnah, and Al-
Rakaya in the Hama province.

The Russian Air Force targeted ISIS with 11 airstrikes over
Al- Raqqah while targeting electrical grids outside it, two
airstrikes over Shadadi-Hasakah highway, and three
airstrikes in Al-Mayadeen province.

The primary ISIS military base in Tabaqa Military Airport
was also attacked, with the barracks being destroyed in two
airstrikes. ISIS weapons supply depot in Al-Ajrawi Frams
was bombed and its primary headquarters in Tabaqa
National Hospital was heavily damaged in a Russian
airstrike.

There have been reports that Herzbollah and Iranian
fighters were preparing major ground offensives to be
coordinated with Russian airstrikes.

According to CNN, the Russian defense ministry said its

soldiers bombed nine ISIS positions near the groups de facto capital in Raqqa. At least 11 were killed in an alleged double strike by Russia in Syria's Idlib province.

In October 2015, according to Russian officials, four warships from the Russian Navy's Caspian Flotilla launched 26 3M-14T from KALIBR-NK system cruise missiles that hit 11 targets within Syrian territory. The missiles passed through Iranian and Iraqi airspace in order to reach their targets at a distance of about 1,500 kilometers 930 miles

Russia claimed all its missiles hit their targets. Iran denied any missile crash on its territory. Iranian defense minister sees this as another plot by the West.

On 8 October 2015, the number of air raids increased to over 60 a day and lasted for two days. The Russian defense ministry announced in that same week that 60 ISIS targets had been hit killing about 300 militants. One of the raid targeted a Liwa al-Haqq base in the Al-Raqqah area using 500KR precision-guided bombs, in which two senior ISIS commanders and 200 militants were killed.

Another attack destroyed a former prison near Aleppo that was used by ISIS as a base and ammunition depot, also killing many militants. Rebel training centers in the Latakia and Idlib provinces were hit as well.

The ISIS militants made advances in the Aleppo area on 9 October, capturing several villages including Tal Qrah, Tal Sousin, ANS Kfar Qares,

When this happened, the Russian and Syrian troops formed a joint coalition to attack the rebels in Aleppo.

After the Paris and Sinai attacks, the Russian forces targeted ISIS in Raqqa, Deir ez-Zor , Aleppo and Idlib. The mass cruise missile dtrike carried out against ISIS in the above-mentioned area resulted in the death of more than 600 militants according to the ministry.

During its fight against insurgency in Syria, a Russian Sukhoi Su 24 strike aircraft was shot down by a Turkish Air Force F-16 on 24 November 2015. The pilot was shot and killed by rebels.

According to Turkey, the planes disregarded multiple warnings and were fired upon by Turkish F-16s patrolling the area. After the Turkish fire, one of the planes left Turkish airspace and crashed into Syrian territory.

The Russian Ministry denied that any of their planes had violated Turkey's airspace, claiming they had been flying south of the Yayladagi province.

The incident led to tensions between Turkey and Russia over alleged repeated violations of Turkish airspace by Russian military jets.

However, Russia responded by deploying additional air defense weapons in the area and accompany its bombers with fighter jets.

Later in November, Russian aircraft were reported to have struck targets in the Syrian Idlib province, including the town of Ariha that had been captured by the Army of Conquest 6 months' prior causing multiple casualties on the ground.

CEASEFIRE TALKS

In early February 2016, the formal start of the United Nation mediated Geneva Syria peace talks and the opposition's protestations notwithstanding, the Syrian government carried on with its offensive operations in the Aleppo.

Other Arab countries like Saudi Arabia, Turkey have asked Russia to stop bombing opposition forces in Syria due to the peace talks, but Russia said that it will not stop its air strikes until the terrorist groups like ISIL and Jabhat al-Nusra are defeated.

On 26 February 2016, the United Nations Security Council has adopted a resolution that demands a cooperation and cease-fire between the fighters in Syria.

Some of the European countries have accepted refugees,

especially Germany, but is just accepting these people going to solve the problem in Syria?

These refugees think Europe is a paradise, but unfortunately they get here and realize that "it is not a bed of roses". Most of them are kept in refugee camps and suffer a lot of anti-racial attacks and some of them have complained of being mishandled in their various camps. Many say that they are afraid to go out at night and therefore have to go out in groups in order to ensure safety.

When the war started the world leaders did not pay so much attention to the situation in Syria until the war escalated. At that time many might have asked themselves "would the Syrian war promote their national interests" take a look at the effect of negligence of four years? Politicians are overwhelmed with the refugee crisis in the Middle East and Europe.

I believe Kissinger's methods would have played a key role to hinder the war from escalating to its present position. The initiation of dialogue with Russia to formulate common diplomatic strategies than working against each other would have yielded positive results because this war is actually a tribal conflict against the ancient structure. Also other conflicts, which I have explained in detail like the Libyan Second Civil War has also gone beyond control. Overthrowing Gadhafi and living the rebuilding of the nation to its citizens did not yield any positive results. Today we see a divided country due to tribal differences and this has led to the death of many innocent citizens.

THE ISLAMIC STATE-ISIS

The Islamic state of Iraq and Syria is a Salafi Jihadist militant group that follows an Islamic fundamentalist, Wahhabi doctrine of Sunni Islam just like the Boko Haram in Nigeria. It proclaimed a worldwide caliphate in June 2014 and claims religious, political and military authority over all Muslims worldwide.

It has taken over territories in Iraq and Syria, where it enforces its sharia law. ISIS affiliates control small areas of Lybia, Nigeria, Afghanistan and operate in other parts of the world, including North Africa and South Asia.

ISIS gained recognition in early 2014 when it drove the Iraqi government forces out of key cities in its Western Iraq, followed by the capture of Mosul and the Sinjar massacre.

This prompted a renewed US military action in the country. The group has conducted ground attacks on both government forces and rebel factions in Syria.

The number of fighters the group commands in Iraq and Syria was estimated by the CIA at 31,000 with foreign fighters accounting for around two thirds, while ISIS leaders claim 40,000 fighters with the majority being Iraqi and Syrian nationals.

This group has beheaded soldiers, civilians, journalists and aid workers. The United Nations holds ISIS responsible for human rights abuses, war crimes and destruction of world heritage sites.

Islamic leaders have condemned ISIS ideology and actions, saying that the group are not following the path of true Islam and that its actions do not reflect the religious teachings.

In late January 2015, it was reported that ISIS members had entered the European Union and disguised themselves as civilian refugees who were emigrating from the war zones of Iraq.

An ISIS representative claimed that ISIS had successfully smuggled 4,000 fighters and that the smuggled fighters were planning attacks in Europe in retaliation for the airstrikes' carried out against ISIS targets in Iraq and Syria.

In 2015 and 2016, ISIS claimed responsibility for a number of high profile terrorist attacks outside Iraq and Syria, including a mass shooting at Tunisian tourist resort killing 38 European tourists, the Suruc bombing in Turkey 33 leftist and pro-Kurdish activities killed, the Tunisian National Museum attack 24 foreign tourists and Tunisian killed, the Sana mosque bombings 142 Shia civilians killed, the crash of Metrojet Flight 9268 (224 killed, mostly Russian tourists, the bombings in Ankara, 102 pro-Kurdish and leftist activists killed), the bombings in Beirut 43 shia civilians killed, the November 2015 Paris attacks (130 civilians killed, the killing of Jaafar Mohammed Saad, the governor of Aden, and the 2016 Istanbul bombing 11 foreign tourists were killed.

ISIS relies mostly on captured weapons and weapons from government and opposition forces fighting in the Syrian Civil war and during fighting in the Syrian Civil War and during the post US withdrawal Iraqi insurgency.

According to a study, ISIS finances itself through funds from the occupation of territory including the control of banks, oil, gas, taxation, extortion, robbery of economic assets, kidnapping for ransom.

They receive donations from Saudi Arabia and Gulf States often disguised as meant for humanitarian aid, stolen artifacts are smuggled into Turkey and Jordan and sold for millions of dollars. They make money through trafficking of Afghan heroin through its territory.

They also receive monetary support from extremists who leave their country to train in Iraq and Syria.

EFFORTS TO STOP ISIS AND THE CONFLICT IN THE MIDDLE EAST

The French president at the G-20 summit last year said that "we are united and allies are prepared to wage war against the ISIS terrorist group":

So far, many ISIS primary source of revenue and most of its base have come under attack, which has helped to weaken it from expanding and help intercept any kind of support they receive from individuals and other extremist organizations.

The America and European countries believe so much in bombs and ground forces. It is like everyone is competing against each other to show off their weapons of mass destruction.

Can you imagine a world, where every time you leave your house, you have doubts that you might never come back? Just because someone is trying to impose its selfish and psychopathic ideas on the whole world.

I do not think sending more military forces to Iraq will solve this problem properly, neither do I encourage any government to negotiate with terrorists, but with the present situation in the Middle East, America and Europe, they have no choice, but to come together and try to initiate a diplomatic coalition with the Arab Muslim leaders in countries like Jordan, Iran, Turkey, Saudi Arabia, Lebanon and even Russia, who everyone presently sees as an outcast.

4
CONCLUSION

Diplomats play their roles, mainly in the areas of conflict prevention, management and resolution, as well as in foreign policy formulation and execution. These areas involve negotiations, "shuttle" diplomacy, and treaty making. The Diplomatic mission is a very tasking duty to the fatherland, and yet must take into recognition the fact that all humanity is one family. This knowledge must inform all patriotic posturing and diplomatic expertise of diplomats. Henry Kissinger missed this point, and this omission and its consequences still hunt him today as students humiliate him when they can, while many people are seeking opportunities to sue him to court and bring him to justice. Diplomats have to be careful when in service, and advise their governments aright in this direction because when the chips are down, they will bear full responsibility for their actions, and not the government or governments that may have also left office. Henry Kissinger is one of the greatest diplomats of our times. However, it is doubtful if his greatness resounds in more than a few states of the world outside the United

States. He aided US governments to pursue US national interests in such a way that they overwhelmed all sense of justice and fairness, and even over-ran the sovereignty of independent nations, discarding citizens' rights to choose their leaders democracy, and even seeking to over-run the position of continents as in that of the organization of African Unity now African Union over Angola.

Diplomats need to know that the end does not always justify the means, and that international morality, international public opinion, and international humanitarian law now trail perpetrators of war crimes, crimes against humanity and those leaders and their agents who violate human rights with impunity.

Another recommended book by Esther Samson is the Trails of a woman available both in English and German language.

It is a research work, which delineates the challenges, which confront women from different cultural background.

It also explores the dangers female refugees face on their journey to Europe as well as the sexual exploitation of young women by peacekeeping forces in central Africa and many other interesting topics which will broaden your horizon.

Also, revealing true life stories of women and on abuse and other prejudices and lastly the way forward.

REFERENCES

Harold Nicholson, Diplomacy, New York, Oxford University Press, 1963, p. 21. Also see Harvester Wheatsheaf, Theory And Practice of Diplomacy, London, Prentice Hal Pub., 1995.

Femi Adegbolu, Topics And Issues In International Relations, Abeokuta Ogun State, Babcock University Press, 2006, p. 51. Also see Normad Palmar and Howard Porkins, International Relations, Pennsylvania, University of Pennsylvania, 2005.

See R. Seligman, Encyclopedia of The Social Sciences, vol. 3, New York, MacMillan Pub. 1967.

V.B.E. Abia, Contemporary Issues In International Relations, Lagos, Concepts Pub. Ltd, 2000.

Lewis Coser, The Functions of Social Conflict, New York, The Free Press, quoted in OBC Nwolise, The Nigeria Police In International Peace Keeping Under The Nations, Ibadan, Spectrum Books Ltd, 2004, P.1.

See J.W. Burton, "Resolution of Conflict", in International Studies Quarterly Journal, Vol. 16, Cambridge, Cambridge University Press, 1972.

Sir Ernest Satow, Guide To Diplomatic Practice, vol. 2, London 1922.

Henry Kissinger, Diplomacy, New York, Simon and Shuster Publishers, 1994.

See The Foreign Service, Series 6, Washington DC, Government Printing Office, August 11, 1946.

See Nicholson Harold, The Congress of Vienna, New York, !946, pp 164-165.

See Evi Kurz, Bad Kissingen, London, Orion Publishing, 2005

See Henry Kissinger, White House Years, Boston, Simon and Shuster Pub. 1979.

For details, see Henry Kissinger, Years of Renewal, New York, Simon and Shuster Pub. 1999.

Sourced from internet: http://www.nobleprize.org accessed 16 March, 2009.

On net, http://www.msn.kissinger.com accessed March 20, 2009.
Internet sourced at http://www.wikipedia.com accessed on March 22, 2009.

See http://www.US/southasiancrisis.com accessed April 5, 2009.

See http://www.nowsbbc.co.uk accessed April 5, 2009.

See http://www.whitehouse.gov.edu accessed April 9, 2009. Also see http://www.rawstory.com/news/1973 accessed April 12, 2009.

For details see, Richard Thorton, The Nixon – Kissinger Years, New York, Brown Publishing, 1976.

See Richard Thorton, Ibid; and Christopher Hitchens, The Trial of Henry Kissinger, London, Verso Books, 2001.

This Method Involved Flying Back and Forth Several

Times Between Israel and Egypt, Working as a Third Party
Mediator.

For example see Hitchens Christopher, The Trial of Henry
Kissinger, London, Verso Books, 2001.
See The Guardian on Saturday, December 6, 2003.

See "Iraq War" www.britannica.com/event/Iraq War.
March 3, 2016.

See http:// Wikipedia.org/wiki/Wahhabism.   March 5,
2016.

See www.allafrican.com. March 4 and 5, 2016.

See www.bbc.african.com March 6, 2016.

See www.worldbank.org

See http://wikipedia.org/islamic state. March 6, 2016.

See http://wiki/Russian military intervention in Syrian
Civil War March 8, 2016.

**See http://wiki/Libyan Civil War (2014-Present) March
8, 2016**

ANOTHER RECOMMENDED BOOK

Another recommended book by Esther Samson is Trials of a Woman. A book which delineates the challenges that confronts women from different cultural background worldwide.

www.ingramcontent.com/pod-product-compliance
Lightning Source LLC
Chambersburg PA
CBHW030537290526
45786CB00004B/1750